GRADE

6

The Syllabus of Examination:
requirements, especially tho
sight-reading. Attention sho
Notices on the inside front c
of any changes.

GW00419463

The syllabus is obtainable f
The Associated Board of tl
14 Bedford Square, London WC1B 3JG (please send a
stamped addressed C5 (162mm × 229mm) envelope).

In examination centres outside the UK, information and
syllabuses may be obtained from the Local Representative.

CONTENTS

Where appropriate, pieces in this volume have been checked with original source material
and edited as necessary for instructional purposes. Fingering, phrasing, bowing,
metronome marks and the editorial realization of ornaments (where given) are for
guidance but are not comprehensive or obligatory.

**DO NOT
PHOTOCOPY
© MUSIC**

Alternative pieces for this grade

Music origination by Jack Thompson.
Cover by Økvik Design.
Printed in England by Halstan & Co. Ltd,
Amersham, Bucks.

7-95

Adagio
Second movement from Sonata in B flat, Op. 9 No. 3

A:1

Edited by
Richard Jones

HÜLLMANDEL

Nicolas-Joseph Hüllmandel (1756–1823), born at Strasbourg in the same year as Mozart, settled in Paris in 1776 but fled to London upon the outbreak of the French Revolution. He published 21 sonatas for piano or harpsichord with the accompaniment of a violin (rather than vice versa), though in the present slow movement the violin occupies the foreground. As befits an expressive slow movement the dynamics are perhaps best kept restricted to sub-*forte* levels and conceived as relative to each other. The signs *fp* and *sf* are accents whose force depends on context: they should not be taken literally, nor do they have any necessary bearing on the prevailing dynamic level of the passage concerned.

Source: *Trois Sonates*, Op. 9 (Paris, 1787).

© 2000 by The Associated Board of the Royal Schools of Music

Allegro

Fourth movement from Sonata in G, Book 4, No. 6

Edited by
Richard Jones

SENAILLÉ

Jean Baptiste Senaillé (*c.*1688–1730) took his father's place as violinist in the 24 Violons du Roi in 1713 and published no fewer than 50 sonatas for violin and continuo between 1710 and 1727. He was one of the first French violinist-composers to adopt the Italian sonata style. All dynamics are editorial suggestions only. The sign **+** (e.g. bar 3) is a very widespread method of indicating a shake or trill in Baroque music, particularly that written for violin or flute.

Source: *Quatrième Livre de Sonates* (Paris, 1721).

A:3

Siciliana and Allegro

First and second movements from Sonata in A minor, Op. 4 No. 1

Edited by
Richard Jones

STANLEY

John Stanley (1712–86), an English organist and composer who was blind from the age of two, published 14 Solos (sonatas) for violin or flute and continuo, Opp. 1 and 4, in 1740 and 1745. All dynamics, slurs and articulation marks are editorial suggestions only.

Source: *Six Solos*, Op. 4 (London, J. Johnson, 1745).

AB 2750

B:1

Sérénade
Op. 124

BÉRIOT

pour Claude Roland-Manuel

B:2 Berceuse sur le nom de Gabriel Fauré

RAVEL

In 1922 Maurice Ravel (1875–1937) was commissioned to write this piece for a special issue of the magazine *La Revue musicale,* published in honour of his teacher Gabriel Fauré (1845–1924). About Ravel's contribution Fauré wrote '…it touched me deeply and I thank you for it with all my heart'. The Berceuse also celebrated the birth of Claude Roland-Manuel, the son of Roland Alexis Manuel Lévy, Ravel's friend, pupil and fellow composer.

AB 2750

Allegro molto

First movement from Sonata in D, Op. 137 No. 1, D. 384

Edited by
Richard Jones

SCHUBERT

B:3

Schubert's set of three sonatas for violin and piano were written within a few weeks in the spring of 1816, when he was 19. First published posthumously by Schubert's champion Anton Diabelli in 1836 under the spurious title 'sonatinas', they have since become among his best-known and most popular chamber works.

Sources: autograph draft, 'Sonate pour Pianoforte et Violons' [sic]; second autograph of piano part only; *Drei Sonatinen*, Op. 137 (Vienna, Diabelli, 1836).

12

13

AB 2750

C:1

An Evening in the Village

No. 5 from *Ten Easy Pieces*

Arranged by
Tibor Fülep

BARTÓK

In the summer of 1907 Béla Bartók (1881–1945) travelled round the villages of Transylvania collecting ancient folk music. *An Evening in the Village* (1908) reflects the pentatonic sound and alternation between *rubato* and *non rubato* of some of the folk music that he heard there.

Canción Valenciana

No. 5 from *Siete Canciones Valencianas*

RODRIGO

C:2

C:3

Fantasia on Greensleeves

Arranged by
Michael Mullinar

VAUGHAN WILLIAMS

Fantasia on Greensleeves, originally scored for strings, harp and one or two flutes, is an adaptation by Ralph Greaves of parts of Vaughan Williams' work *Sir John in Love* (1924–28), a light-hearted opera in four acts. The opera contains a number of folk songs including 'Greensleeves', and 'Lovely Joan' upon which the middle section of the Fantasia is based.

© Oxford University Press 1944
Reproduced by permission. All enquiries for this piece apart from the examinations should be addressed to Oxford University Press, Great Clarendon Street, Oxford, OX2 6DP.

handwritten: Bb 234123012/123412/12-1234 4321-321-3214 e\5

Grade 6

handwritten: 234123 4 123412 34

			separate bows						slurred						
Major Scales									*seven notes to a bow*						
	Db **Major**	2 Octaves	✓	✓	✓				✓	✓	✓				
	F **Major**	2 Octaves	✓	✓	✓				✓	✓		✓			
	F# **Major**	2 Octaves	✓	✓	✓				✓	✓	✓				
	A **Major**	3 Octaves	✓	✓	✓				✓	✓	✓				
	Bb **Major**	3 Octaves	✓												

handwritten left: 232123 123412343
handwritten left: 1230123012-123412 12-1234 3 321-321-321

Minor Scales			HARM						*seven notes to a bow* MEL						
(*melodic* and *harmonic*)	C# **Minor**	2 Octaves	✓						✓						
	F **Minor**	2 Octaves	✓	✓	✓				✓	✓					
	F# **Minor**	2 Octaves	✓						✓						
	A **Minor**	3 Octaves	✓						✓	✓					
	Bb **Minor**	3 Octaves	✓	✓	✓				✓	✓					

handwritten left: start on 2 all in 3rd pos
handwritten left: 1234 123 1234 1234

Chromatic Scales		TOP							*four or six notes to a bow*						
	on Ab	2 Octaves *01234*	✓	✓	✓				✓						
	on B	2 Octaves *012·12234*		✓	✓				✓						
	on C	2 Octaves *012·123·12*		✓											

handwritten left: Basic pattern 012-1234
handwritten left: starts on 2
handwritten left: starts on 3

Major Arpeggios									*six notes (two-octave arpeggios) and three notes (three-octave arpeggios) to a bow*						
	Db **Major**	2 Octaves	✓	✓	✓				✓	✓	✓				
	F **Major**	2 Octaves	✓	✓	✓					✓					
	F# **Major**	2 Octaves	✓	✓	✓						✓				
	A **Major**	3 Octaves	✓	✓	✓				✓	✓	✓				
	Bb **Major**	3 Octaves	✓		✓				✓						

handwritten left: 2 4 2 1 3 1 4
handwritten left: 131-1314
handwritten left: 131-131-1314
handwritten left: 2 4 6 2 1-132-13431 41

Minor Arpeggios									*six notes (two-octave arpeggios) and three notes (three-octave arpeggios) to a bow*						
	C# **Minor**	2 Octaves	✓	✓					✓	✓					
	F **Minor**	2 Octaves	✓	✓						✓					
	F# **Minor**	2 Octaves	✓	✓						✓					
	A **Minor**	3 Octaves	✓						✓	✓					
	Bb **Minor**	3 Octaves	✓	✓					✓	✓					

handwritten left: as major

Dominant Sevenths									*four notes to a bow*						
	in C	2 Octaves *3*	✓	✓					✓						
	in D	2 Octaves *4*	✓	✓					✓						
	in Eb	2 Octaves	✓	✓					✓						

handwritten left: 0202 3 1312 resolve on
handwritten left: 131 3020 23
handwritten left: 202413134

Diminished Sevenths									*four notes to a bow*						
	on G	2 Octaves	✓	✓					✓						
	on A	2 Octaves	✓	✓					✓						

handwritten left: 0 2 3 1 3 3 02 Forward BACK
handwritten left: 3 13 0 2413
handwritten left: Forward Back

			S W W S S W						*refer to syllabus for format*						
Double-Stop Scale	in Bb **Major**	1 8ve *in sixths*	✓	✓											

handwritten bottom: 1 2 3 4 1 2 3 4 Bottom Top Both
handwritten bottom: 0 1 2 3 0 1 2 3

Printed by
Halstan & Co. Ltd., Amersham, Bucks.

3/00